D1074772

PHYSICAL EDUCATION BRANCH

DEPT. OF EDUCATION SUMMER SCHOOL

London.

INNER LONDON EDUCATION AUTHORITY

MOVEMENT EDUCATION FOR INFANTS

W. F. HOUGHTON, *Education Officer*

THE COUNTY HALL · LONDON · S.E.1

1966

A

teach   GV443. L53 1964

ALSO PUBLISHED BY THE
INNER LONDON EDUCATION AUTHORITY

Educational Gymnastics
No. 4162   3s. 6d. post extra

Published by the Inner London Education Authority
The County Hall, London, S.E.1

Publication No. R4E   4s. 0d. postage extra

FOREWORD

THIS book has been prepared by the Authority's women inspectors of physical education in response to many requests received from teachers who are anxious to have a reference book for guidance in the physical education of infants. All movement has a common analysis. Knowledge of this analysis is a fundamental necessity for all teachers of movement. How they may make use of it in different forms of physical education such as lessons in agility, skills or dance is shown in different sections of this book. Suggestions for lessons and tasks have been included in order to meet the demands for some more detailed help. Setting a task to provide the right situation is not easy for teachers who are inexperienced in this approach and, for this reason, descriptions of tasks have been worded as teachers might present them to the children. They are intended as a guide, but, as understanding of the work grows, teachers will be able to observe and assess the needs of the children and devise their own tasks accordingly. The examples given should not be used as a series of exercises. Realisation of the value of this work in the development of the whole person will become increasingly evident as teachers observe a child's thoughtful work, growing confidence, greater skill and surprised delight in some new discovery.

w. 3. Houghton

Education Officer.

A*

929301

EDUCATION

CONTENTS

PAGE

CHAPTER I

INTRODUCTION TO INFANTS' PHYSICAL EDUCATION .. 7

    Safety 8
    The Analysis of Movement 9
    The Programme 12

CHAPTER II

MOVEMENT TRAINING AND AGILITY LESSONS 13

  Early Stages 13
    Plan of Lessons 13
    Suggestions for Movement Training .. 15
    Suggestions for Apparatus Work 16

  Progression from the early stages 19
    Plan of Lesson 19
    Transference of Weight 20
    Stages of Development in the use of
      Apparatus 25
    Examples of Tasks on Apparatus 26

  Diagram of Analysis of Movement for the
  Agility Lesson .. .. facing 26

  Movement Ideas 26
    Lifting different parts of the body high .. 27
    Moving with feet together and far apart .. 29
    Moving with the hands near to the feet or
      away from the feet 30
    Curling and Stretching 32
    Twisting and Turning 33
    Shape 35

CHAPTER III

THE OUTDOOR LESSON 37

Early Stages 38
    Suggestions of activities 38
Progression from the early stages 39
Diagram of Analysis of Movement for the
    Outdoor lesson .. .. *facing* 40
Development of Skills 40
    Skills without Apparatus 40
    Skills with Apparatus 41
Examples of Lessons 46

CHAPTER IV

DANCE 49

Early Stages 50
Analysis of movement with reference to Dance.. 52
Diagram of Analysis of Movement for the Dance
    lesson .. .. *facing* 52
Progression from the early stages 53
    Planning a Lesson 53
    Some Movement Ideas 54
    Development of the Movement Idea of
        Strong and Light 54
    Partner and Group Work 57
    Accompaniment 58
Examples of Lessons 60

BIBLIOGRAPHY 63

CHAPTER I

INTRODUCTION TO INFANTS' PHYSICAL EDUCATION

The keynote of all physical education activities should be enjoyment and purpose. If children have not attended a nursery class on entering the Infant school they may have little previous experience on which to draw. The opportunities which a hall or playground provide and the uses to which small and large apparatus can be put will in the main be unknown to the children. They will first need to explore, with a sense of adventure which the word implies, their new environment. The aim of the teacher is first, therefore, to see that this can be done with safety and consideration for others. The next stage is for the teacher to guide the children to discover the ways in which they can use their bodies and to find out what they can do with various pieces of apparatus. This stage gradually passes into one in which the teacher guides the children's experiments and activities into more definite channels. She helps them to develop their playlike activities into more purposeful and skilful ones. In this way they can begin to acquire the basic skills on which games, gymnastics and dance are based in the Junior school.

The most successful teachers know how long they should leave the children to experiment freely in the handling of apparatus and when to give coaching in fundamental skills or to set tasks. Tasks are set in lessons in order to encourage each individual child to work within his own capacity and, by finding different ways of solving a task, to gain a wider experience of movement. These tasks, whilst limiting the children's field of experiment, stimulate their sense of purpose and inventiveness. This ensures that a limited number of favourite activities are not continued indefinitely. If the teacher gives insufficient time for the unguided and experimental period in the handling and use of apparatus, the children will lose their zest and joyousness and may, at a later stage, lack the confidence necessary for more advanced work. On the other hand, if the teacher prolongs this period the children's work gradually loses its purposefulness, the class puts little effort into the work, takes no pride in achievement, disciplinary problems begin to arise and the lessons take on the nature of ' Playtime '. Recognising that each child is an individual, with his own particular movement potentialities and creative powers, the teacher will wish to create a framework in which each child can develop these to the full and be allowed to work at the pace and in the manner most appropriate to his skill and aptitude.

For all physical education lessons children should be suitably clad. For indoor work, if the floor is clean and splinter-proof the children should be barefooted and wear only pants or knickers. In the playground plimsolls are essential and a pullover may be required. Girls should not wear dresses or skirts as these impede movement and the habit of tucking them into their knickers is not hygienic.

Both indoors and in the playground the lessons should begin as soon as the children have changed; waiting in draughts at classroom doors or in the corridor should be avoided and lessons should start promptly and be lively and active. Whenever possible the children should change in the classroom and be trained to leave their clothing tidily on a desk or chair. These good habits are as important as the active work in the lesson and time is not wasted in persevering with this social training.

SAFETY

Safety must be the first consideration at all times and the following points are of great importance.

1. Accommodation

- (*a*) The choice of activity must be governed by the size of the hall.
- (*b*) The floor should be kept as clean and splinter-proof as possible and should not be slippery.
- (*c*) All furniture, which cannot be removed from the hall, must be placed safely or stacked in suitable positions, freeing the largest space possible.
- (*d*) The teacher should note the likely ' danger points ' (sharp corners, hot-plates, etc.) and guard against them.

(e) At no time should walls be used as finishing marks for races.

(f) When working in a sloping playground, activities such as running and jumping, should be organised across and not up and down the slope.

2. Clothing

Suitable clothing should be worn (see page 8). Because of the inability to grip the floor firmly and the danger of slipping, neither the wearing of socks without shoes nor the use of hard-soled shoes should be allowed.

3. Agility Apparatus

(a) Each piece of apparatus must be in sound condition, e.g. no splinters, torn surfaces or stitching, highly polished leather, unsteady supports, etc.

(b) The children should receive careful instruction in the handling of apparatus in order to prevent damage to themselves, the apparatus or the floor. It is a common practice for the apparatus to be put up and to remain out for a session, classes using it in rotation. All classes should be trained, with the assistance of the teacher, to make minor alterations and adjustments to suit their requirements.

(c) Adequate space should be allowed around each grouping of apparatus so that collisions between children working on different sections are avoided.

(d) Mats should be provided whenever the teacher asks for a jump from a height, otherwise they should be placed wherever the task calls for their use.

(e) Any improvised apparatus such as platforms, boxes, tables, etc., must be strong and stable. A check should be made for any splinters or projecting nails, hooks, etc. (Chairs should not be used except to support canes or hoops, which should be free to fall when touched.)

THE ANALYSIS OF MOVEMENT

Teachers should have an understanding of the following simple analysis of movement, but it must be realized that in the main it is the teacher who requires the knowledge and not the child. A young child is natural and spontaneous and in order to preserve this the teacher should use her knowledge in the simplest possible way to give the children experience in feeling different ways of moving.

The body is the agent or instrument of movement. If an instrument is to be well and fully used a knowledge of its parts and its potentialities is necessary. The child therefore should be made aware of one part of the body in relation to other parts or to the whole and the term ' body awareness ' is associated with these experiences.

Movements of the human body may be functional, serving a practical purpose such as surmounting obstacles and handling objects or it may be of an art form as in creative dance. There are certain factors common to all movement and these are defined as Weight, Space, Time and Flow, and it is upon these factors that this analysis is based. The sensation a child receives from a movement differs each time the emphasis placed on any one of these factors is altered. The movement potentialities of the body are used to the greatest advantage when the child can apply the appropriate blending of the Weight, Space, Time and Flow factors to any action.

Weight

The term ' weight ' here covers not only the use made of the weight of the body but also the muscular action. Together these enable the child to move with varying degrees of strength or lightness. Relaxation is achieved by the ' letting go ' of muscular tension. This too can vary in degree and when complete the muscles are in a state of rest. In the agility lesson the muscular effort is used to assist the body to negotiate obstacles effectively and serves a functional purpose. In dance weight is used to stress accents, to help in phrasing and to simulate strength and lightness.

Space

1. PERSONAL SPACE

The body is surrounded by space into which, from a stationary base, it can be extended in all directions and at all levels.

2. GENERAL SPACE

As soon as the body begins to travel it moves into the general space. When travelling, movements can be made in different directions, forwards, backwards, sideways, upwards and downwards. High levels can be reached with stretches, leaps and bounds, and low levels by bending, curling up or rolling on the floor.

As a movement is made in space, the body can assume or move through a specific shape; the long extended, the small compact and rounded, or the wide shape. Every movement describes a certain path in space. The path followed between two points, either by a part of the body or the whole body, will be flexible or direct.

Time

Any movement uses a quantity of time: it may be quick using little time or slow using much time. The speed of the movement need not be uniform throughout and variations of time may be developed into a rhythmic pattern. The quality of time is shown by suddenness or sustainment in movement.

Flow

The flow of movement can be ' bound ' or ' free '. A movement which can be stopped or held without difficulty at any stage in the action is termed ' bound '. A movement which is difficult to stop suddenly is termed ' free '; this has its place in dance but because of the greater need to control the body in the agility lesson ' bound ' flow is more often used.

The careful observation of any movement will show that with this analysis there are variations of each of these factors within the movement, i.e. TIME—there will be changes of time, this may alter from sudden to sustained, the speed may increase or decrease; WEIGHT—parts of the action may be light, other parts may be strong; SPACE—parts of the movement may be high others low and a change of direction may be made; FLOW—the fluent changing of these effort qualities gives harmony and ease of performance. The right effort at the right moment gives skill and effectiveness.

Individuals differ greatly in mental and physical attributes and so each will use the movement factors in different but equally effective ways.

11

THE PROGRAMME

The aim should be a daily lesson of some form of physical education. The distribution of the various types of lesson will obviously vary from school to school depending on facilities, availability of the hall and the time of year. However, the programme should include, if possible, the following:

I. One movement training lesson finishing with agility work using small apparatus as obstacles.
II. Two agility lessons using large apparatus.
III. One skills lesson using small apparatus.
IV. One dance lesson.

Each of these lessons caters for a different type of movement and the purpose for which it is used. In the movement training lesson and that taken on the agility apparatus the movement involves different ways of rolling, which is the basis of safety training. Through this, as well as weight bearing on the hands and running and jumping, the child learns to manage his or her body when negotiating obstacles. These two kinds of lessons should take place in the hall where the floor surface is more suited to this kind of movement.

The skills lesson with small apparatus will give the child experience in handling apparatus and the opportunity for the acquisition of skills which are mainly concerned with the co-ordination of eyes, hands and feet, e.g. games and athletics. As space is an essential factor in a lesson of this kind, it is better taken in the playground.

Finally the dance lesson will give the child the chance to use movement expressively. Unhampered by obstacles and objects, he or she will be able to give free reign to the imagination and can learn to interpret ideas through movement.

Teachers should be prepared to adapt the programme and in good weather lessons should be taken in the playground with the emphasis on the skills lesson.

CHAPTER II

MOVEMENT TRAINING AND AGILITY LESSONS

The work in the movement training lessons is taken not only for safety but also to give material which will stimulate the children to new ideas on the apparatus. The two types of lessons are very closely inter-linked and one is essential to the other. For this reason the children should have the chance to experiment with movement ideas while working on the floor before applying these ideas to the large apparatus. The lesson in which small apparatus is used for obstacles is perhaps the best way of showing children how interesting and imaginative their movement can be with quite simple arrangements of canes, hoops and individual mats. Later these arrangements can become the supplementary groups for such apparatus as the London Agility on which the whole class cannot work at a time. If the time-table or facilities do not allow for a separate movement training lesson, it is essential that some work of this type is taken prior to the children using the apparatus. Suggestions of lesson plans and material that can be used both for the early and later stages of the work, follow.

EARLY STAGES

PLAN OF LESSON

Opening Activity

Simple running movements with emphasis on spacing and response.

Movement Training

Two or three activities in which the children gain experience in moving on different parts of the body in a variety of ways.

Climax

Either—Use of small apparatus as obstacles

        (*a*) individually with a similar piece for each child.

        (*b*) with varied settings at which small groups of children work.

Or   —Agility apparatus supplemented where necessary by (*a*) or (*b*) above.

The children will learn to manage themselves safely on the floor and on apparatus if given the opportunity to climb over, under and through obstacles of various heights and types. In the movement training the main stress will be on the natural movements of walking, running, skipping, hopping, jumping and rolling, and on the good use of the floor space. In addition, the children will enjoy and learn from the sensations they feel when briefly experiencing the various aspects of movement. They will, in fact, be learning ' a little about a lot ' and no movement idea should be pursued for too long at any one time.

The agility apparatus gives opportunity for such natural movements as climbing and jumping, but before the children use it in these early stages the teacher must be sure that they will respond to her instructions, that they can space themselves sensibly and will not interfere with other children. In the main, apparatus will consist of the London Agility apparatus, Essex apparatus, tripods, mats, drama boxes, platforms and small apparatus used as obstacles. The work will take the same form whichever type of apparatus is used. When first using the climbing apparatus, children should be given the opportunity to explore the apparatus and find the various ways of gripping and taking their weight on it in order to move with confidence and safety.

At first the teacher will have in mind her main aims of spacing, response, safety and enjoyment. Running is both natural and enjoyable to young children and through this activity the teacher can establish these basic essentials. The children may be told to run anywhere and be given practice at stopping at the teacher's word. Spacing may be encouraged by using such phrases as ' Find all the spaces ', ' Go by yourself ', etc. It is important at this stage that guidance is given in running softly and safely.

14

The feeling of putting the feet down softly on to the floor may be achieved by working on a contrast of movement. By making the feet stiff and hard they can be banged on the floor and by making them loose they can be put softly on the floor. In addition to running, other ways of moving may be explored.

SUGGESTIONS FOR MOVEMENT TRAINING

1. Run anywhere. Which part of you is touching the floor? Now move in different ways with your feet still touching the floor. (The children may skip, hop, gallop, slip, jump, etc.—one of these activities may then be tried by all the class.)

2. Run round the hall (indicate direction) and when you see a space run in to it and jump as high as you can.

3. Stand in a space, practise jumping coming down softly.

4. Run and jump coming down as softly as you can.

5. Move about in any way you like with your feet only touching the floor, making yourself very small and then very big.

6. Put your hands down on the floor (lift your head up) and find different ways in which you can travel with your hands and feet on the floor. Move softly.

7. Travel with your hands and feet on the floor (e.g. with front towards the floor, with back towards the floor, running with feet, jumping with feet, kicking legs in the air, etc.).

8. Travel with your hands and feet on the floor, going forwards, backwards, and sideways.

9. Travel with your hands and feet on the floor, taking up a little space and then a lot of space.

10. Travel with your hands and feet on the floor, with your hands close to your feet and then with your hands far from your feet.

11. Curl up in a little ball on the floor. Which part of you is touching the floor? Now curl up again with a different part touching.

12. Stretch out on the floor, then curl up. Now find another way of stretching out.

13. Curl up in a little ball on the floor; roll along.

14. You have been rolling in a little ball. Can you roll stretched out?

15.   Can you find another way of travelling with your body on the floor?

16.   Travel with your body on the floor, taking up a little space and then a lot of space.

17.   Travel slowly and then quickly with only your feet touching the floor.

18.   Travel slowly and then quickly with your feet and hands touching the floor.

19.   Travel about the floor on different parts of your body.

20.   Put your hands on the floor, keep your head up, kick or jump your legs in the air and bring your feet down in a new place.

21.   Travel with your seat nearest the ceiling.

SUGGESTIONS FOR APPARATUS WORK

Large Apparatus

At first, the apparatus itself will present a challenge to the children and sufficient time must therefore be given to the free exploratory use of it. To enable the teacher to provide situations in which confidence will continue to grow and new ideas develop, some suggestions for class activities are listed below. The experience gained will probably be incorporated by the children in their free work on the apparatus.

1.   Move about, going under as many pieces of apparatus as you can.

2.   Find different places where you can climb on to the apparatus.

3.   Move about the room using as many pieces of apparatus as you can.

4.   Find different ways of coming off the apparatus.

5.   Move about the apparatus on your hands and feet only.

6.   Move along on top of a piece of apparatus.

7.   Move along on the underside of a piece of apparatus.

8.   Curl up on the apparatus, find another place and stretch out.

9.   Find a place on the apparatus and lift a part of your body high.

10. Find a place on the apparatus, grip tightly and pull yourself close to it, then come down softly.

The teacher should always place herself so that she can observe as many of the children as possible. During the lessons the teacher should give thought and attention to the following important points in training.

1. The children should be well spaced on the apparatus so that they are able to move freely without interference with the work of others.
2. The children should make sure that there is space to land when coming off the apparatus. Once they are down they should move to the side while deciding what to do, so that the space underneath the apparatus is always clear.
3. Training in putting themselves down softly and safely is an essential. When asked by the teacher to come off they should take the shortest route down and this should not be misinterpreted as speed of movement. They should understand clearly that once they are told to finish they do not touch or use the apparatus again.
4. Running across mats presents certain hazards. Children can trip or collide with a child jumping down. Training should make them aware of this. In the same way they should realize that it is safer to bear their weight on some part of their body when going over a fixed pole or plank rather than to leap over it.

Small Apparatus

Small apparatus such as canes, hoops, individual mats, can provide challenging obstacles. The activity of negotiating these obstacles can form the climax of a lesson or supplement the use of the large apparatus. A few suggestions of individual activities and group settings are given below.

Hoops. (Individual)

A hoop is placed on the floor as an obstacle.

1. Run round your hoop. Now find other ways of going round with only your feet touching the floor.
2. Find different ways of going round your hoop with your hands and feet on the floor.

17

3. Move in and out of your hoop making different parts of your body touch the floor.
4. Jump in and out of your hoop. Can you land softly?
5. Curl up in your hoop and stretch out.
6. Move into your hoop and curl up. Now as you come out, can you stretch?

In the same way use can be made of canes and individual mats. It will be seen that the suggested tasks for Movement Training can be applied to these pieces of apparatus.

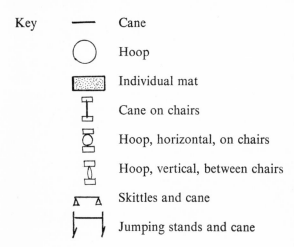

Key   ——   Cane

Hoop

Individual mat

Cane on chairs

Hoop, horizontal, on chairs

Hoop, vertical, between chairs

Skittles and cane

Jumping stands and cane

GROUP SETTINGS

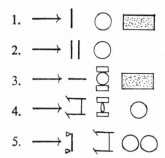

18

The children should be asked to find different ways of travelling over the course provided by these obstacles. The path they travel should at first be indicated by the teacher in order to avoid collisions.

PROGRESSION FROM THE EARLY STAGES

As the work progresses from the early stages it will be found that the lesson takes on a more definite form. This form must be one which satisfies the needs of the children and guides them to learn more about ways of moving (i.e. the WHAT, HOW, WHERE of movement). In the first place children should learn to travel safely and competently from place to place in the room as well as under, over and through apparatus. In doing this they should be encouraged to find varying and purposeful ways in which this may be done. Travelling usually involves the transference of weight from one part of the body to another and it is the use of these different parts which will give variety and interest to their work.

The material for the lessons is given in the form of tasks. These tasks set certain limits and demand thought from the children if they are to find suitable solutions, at the same time they allow for individual difference. A suggested plan of the lesson follows.

PLAN OF LESSON

I. **Opening Activity.** (Limbering and Warming up).

The children should be encouraged to start work immediately they enter the room. This work can take the form of free practice and can include running, hopping, skipping or springing. Definite training in the effective use of the feet and ankles for propulsion and reception of weight should be given.

II. **Movement Training**

The work in this part of the lesson should give the children good experience for situations which they may meet on the

19

apparatus. Therefore they should learn to take their weight (1) on the body (2) on the legs and (3) on the arms. Equal emphasis should be attached to these three aspects and though it may not be possible to cover all in one lesson, the balance should be restored in subsequent ones.

WHOLE BODY

The weight is supported mainly on the parts of the body other than the hands and feet and the children learn to manage and control their bodies both with movements on the spot and travelling over the floor.

WEIGHT SUPPORTED ON HANDS AND FEET

Movements where the weight is taken on the hands and the feet will be encouraged first and when the arms are sufficiently strong greater emphasis will be placed on taking the weight on the hands. (N.B. It is essential to give the children the safety precaution of lifting the head with the chin out to prevent over-balancing.)

LEG WORK

Movements where only the feet touch the ground are included here. Where applicable, propulsion of the body into the air and good reception of weight on landing should be emphasised.

III. **Climax.**—Apparatus Work

In addition to a period of free practice on the apparatus, opportunity should be given for the movement experiences of the earlier part of the lesson to be applied in the use of one section or all sections of the apparatus. The apparatus should be arranged with imagination to allow the children to fulfil any tasks they are set.

TRANSFERENCE OF WEIGHT

As transference of weight is fundamental to locomotion, skill and security in taking the weight safely on the parts chosen should be acquired before other aspects of movement are considered.

To begin with tasks will be simple and will be carried out on the floor. Then it is hoped that apparatus, suitably arranged, will give opportunity for the children to employ their new-found experience and skill in the more difficult situations which the apparatus presents. Once the children are moving freely, easily and confidently on the floor or apparatus, interest and stimulus can be added by the teacher giving further ideas to the children about the manner in which they could vary their travelling, i.e. change of direction or level. The skilled teacher will know from observation of her class which suggestions will be most timely, i.e. if the majority of the class is moving forward, suggest other directions; if movement is slow or static suggest a change of speed.

The following ideas have been compiled to help the teacher to plan lessons with the emphasis firstly on how the children will be transferring their weight. Suggestions for this are given in two groups: those in the first group are simpler than in the second. Some are so simple that, once understood, they can almost immediately be carried out with variations of time, level, etc. The range of possible variations in ‘Where’ or ‘How’ the children may move is indicated on the diagram of the analysis of movement which faces page 26.

As the children become more confident, courageous and adventurous and land from heights and travel at varying speeds, they will be receiving their weight in much more difficult situations and training and practice will be necessary if they are to do so softly and safely. Suggestions in group II are planned to give the children experience which will enable them to receive their weight safely in these more exacting conditions or to save themselves should they fail to do so.

Movement Training—GROUP I

LEG WORK

Transference of weight using the feet only.

    (a) Using different parts of foot—e.g. heel, side of foot, ball, of foot.

    (b) Walking.

    (c) Running.

    (d) Springing from foot to foot or bob jumping.

    (e) Skipping.

    (f) Hopping.

    (g) Galloping.

WHOLE BODY
  (*a*) Curl up with the weight supported on one part of the body. Repeat, finding the different parts on which this can be done.
  (*b*) Travel curled up
        (i) without a roll,
        (ii) with a sideways roll.
  (*c*) (i) Make any shape on any part of the body then gradually curl up.
        (ii) Make any shape on any part of the body, gradually curl up and roll.

WEIGHT SUPPORTED ON THE HANDS AND FEET
Move on the hands and feet.
  (*a*) With face to floor.
  (*b*) With back to floor.
  (*c*) Turning over continuously so that the above (*a*) and (*b*) are combined.
  (*d*) With two feet and one hand.
  (*e*) With one foot and two hands.

WEIGHT SUPPORTED ON THE ARMS
  (*a*) Place your hands firmly on the floor and keep your chin up. Push hard on your arms and then let your feet run round about your hands so that they make patterns on the floor.
  (*b*) Press your hands firmly on the floor and keep your chin well up. Try to take your weight on your hands. You can kick up one leg after the other or lift both with a jump.
  (*c*) As above but increasing the length of time in which the children remain with their weight balanced on their arms before bringing their feet down softly. By using a twist of the hips the feet can be brought down by the side of the hands. (This is a safety precaution in the case of over-balancing.)

APPARATUS
  Activity on the large apparatus forms the climax of these lessons and the movement used in the earlier part of the lesson is designed to give the children experiences which will contribute to the safe, effective and imaginative use of the apparatus. The manner in which the transfer of experience gained from the floor

22

work can best be utilized in relation to the apparatus must be clear in the teacher's mind. Apparatus must be suitably arranged to give opportunities for exploring movement ideas and the children must be helped to appreciate the link between their floor work and their movement on the apparatus.

In many cases the supply of large apparatus will not cater for all members of a class and small apparatus will have to be arranged as obstacles. It is usually found advisable to train the children on a class basis in the methods of using this small apparatus as obstacles. Each child or pair of children having their own hoop, cane or rope with which to carry out the simple task set by the teacher. If this is done the teacher can assure herself that the children understand their task and when this work forms only a part of the climax of the lesson the children should be able to carry on their activities purposefully and will need less attention from the teacher who can concentrate on what is taking place on the large climbing apparatus.

ORGANISATION

At this stage the children will use the apparatus freely, moving from place to place at will if it is all equally challenging: otherwise a loose form of grouping may be required. See pages 25, 26 and 27 for work on apparatus.

Movement Training—GROUP II

LEG WORK

Running, jumping and landing.
- (a) Running and leaping, landing one foot after the other with continuous movement.
- (b) Running, jumping and landing with resilient give of legs and jump up to recover.

WHOLE BODY
- (a) Rolling sideways for a short distance and change to standing,
    regain feet (i) with the help of hands,
    (ii) without the use of the hands.
- (b) Travelling with continuous transference of weight from one part of the body to another.
    N.B.—Draw the analogy that in walking we have only two feet to step with but when using the body there are many

23

different parts on which to take the weight and stepping can be done from the seat to the back to the shoulders, the knees, the side, etc.

(c) From standing the children relax and let go gradually until drawn down to the knees. From this position they continue to fold up until the body is small and low enough to roll over softly on one side into a sideways roll.

(d) As above but touching the floor first with various suitable parts other than the knees.

(e) Find various parts of the body on which it is possible to balance; increase the difficulty of the balance by making the part or parts of the body touching the ground smaller.

(f) As above, but after holding any position begin to curl up and roll over; continue to roll until it is possible for the children to jump up without any pause in the movement.

COMBINED MOVEMENTS

(a) Walking slowly about the room, lower the body gradually, curling and tucking up and putting a suitable part of the body down on to the ground; continue travelling by rolling in a tucked up position.

(b) As above, but continue to roll until it is possible for the children to jump up without any pause in the movement.

(c) As in (a) and (b) above, but gradually increase the speed of travelling from slow walking to walking, slow running to running. The speed must be determined by the ability of the individual child to lower the body softly to the floor.

N.B.—For infants the safest part of the body with which to touch the ground first is the seat or the side of the seat.

WEIGHT SUPPORTED ON THE HANDS AND FEET

(a) Travelling moving both hands together, followed by both feet.

(b) Travelling springing between feet and hands.

WEIGHT SUPPORTED ON THE ARMS

(a) Take the weight on both hands leaving the floor one foot after the other; bring the feet down softly one after the other.

(b) Take the weight on both hands leaving the floor one foot after the other; bring the feet down together.

(*c*) Take the weight on to both hands and leave the floor with both feet together; bring the feet down one after the other.

(*d*) Take the weight on both hands and leave the floor with both feet together; bring the feet down together.

APPARATUS

Suggestions for successive stages in the use and organisation of the apparatus follow.

STAGES OF DEVELOPMENT IN THE USE OF APPARATUS

1. Where there is sufficient apparatus of comparable interest the children are allowed to work at any piece of apparatus of their choice and to move at will from piece to piece, providing that there is no overcrowding or interference with the work of another child.

2. Class activities are set on the theme of the lesson. For this the children move on the floor and at a signal carry out a simple task on the theme of the lesson on the apparatus.

3. The children carry out movement ideas on the theme of the lesson on various pieces of apparatus of their choice.

4. The apparatus is divided into sections to which groups of children are allocated. The children work freely at their section of apparatus until moved to another by the teacher. In deciding when to move her groups the teacher will have to seek a balance between her desire to ensure that the children have adequate time at a piece of apparatus to obtain results, and equal opportunity of using the more challenging apparatus. Working in groups in this way ensures that the children have experience in using and experimenting with all the apparatus.

5. The class is organised in groups but at one or more sections the children are set simple tasks on the theme of the lesson which they may follow for part or for all the time they are at the section.

6. The class is organised in groups but the children are given the path they must follow in using the apparatus, i.e., up the plank and off the stool—or up the stool and down the plank. This method ensures that a child will have uninterrupted use of piece(s) of apparatus on which to carry out a task. In this case the children may (*a*) make their own choice of activity, (*b*) work out a task which has been set on the theme of the lesson.

25

EXAMPLES OF TASKS ON APPARATUS

London Apparatus

1. Using your hands and feet only, travel about the apparatus in as many different ways as you can.
2. Using your hands and any other part of your body except your feet, travel on the apparatus in as many different ways as you can.
3. Find different places on the apparatus where you can hang, travel or swing.

Essex Apparatus

1. Travel up the plank on one part of your body and down the opposite plank on another part of your body.
2. Climb up the stool using hands and feet and come down the plank on a part of your body.
3. Travel half way up the plank on one part of your body, change on to another part and continue up the plank; find a way of coming off the stool.

Canes and Mats

1. Travel over the cane taking your weight on your hands and feet and over the mat with a roll.
2. Travel over the cane with a jump—over the mat with your weight on your hands and feet.

MOVEMENT IDEAS

Once the children are travelling freely and confidently on the floor or apparatus, they should be encouraged to move in different directions and with a change of time. They will then be ready to discover ' What ' the whole body is capable of doing, e.g. can they move curled up or stretched out, can they twist or turn? We have used the term ' Movement Ideas ' for the various actions of the body.

Suggestions for tasks which can be set to the children are given under the headings of the lesson construction. One or two of these may be introduced at first into the floor work of the lesson based on the material given on the previous pages. Later the teacher may base the whole lesson on the one movement idea by choosing a task on it for each section of the lesson plan. The work can be developed in the climax of the lesson by setting tasks similar to those in the movement training at either one or more sections of the apparatus.

I. LIFTING DIFFERENT PARTS OF THE BODY HIGH

Movement Training

WHOLE BODY

TASK 1—When you are standing, your head is lifted higher than any other part of your body. Can you find a way of lifting your feet higher than any other part of you? How many other parts of your body can you lift high?

TASK 2—Can you move with one part lifted high? Find how many ways you can move, each time with a different part high.

TASK 3—Can you move with one part high and then the same part low?

WEIGHT SUPPORTED ON THE ARMS

TASK 1—With your hands and feet on the floor, move about the room lifting one part high, then another part high.

TASK 2—Put your hands down in front of you on the floor and lift your head up. Keeping your hands there, can you jump or kick your legs up so that your feet or seat are lifted high, bringing your feet down softly? As you come down, twist your body so that your feet land at the side of your hands. (The lifting of the head and twisting of the body are safety precautions in case of overbalancing.)

LEG WORK

TASK 1—Run and jump, lifting your head (chest or hands) high.

TASK 2—Run and jump, lift one part of your leg higher than the rest of your leg. (The knee, toe or heel can be lifted.)

TASK 3—Run and jump, lifting one part of your leg high; try to make the other leg go higher, e.g. make one knee go higher than the other.

Apparatus

TASK 1—Grip the apparatus and lift one part high; change your position and lift another part high.

TASK 2—Travel on the apparatus with one part high.

TASK 3—Travel on the apparatus lifting first one part high and then another part high.

ESSEX APPARATUS

TASK 1—Travel up the plank showing one part of your body lifted high. Stand on the stool. Jump off with your head high.

Whenever children are jumping from a height teachers should emphasize the following points:

(a) that the children must land on both feet; (landing on one foot puts too great a strain on the knee and ankle joint),

(b) that the legs and feet must give in order to land softly and safely.

This will apply to any task they use when coming off stools with jumps and is of particular importance when they have been asked to come off with a stretch.

TASK 2—Moving across the plank, taking your weight on your hands, show a part of your body lifted high.

TASK 3—Using the pole, travel from one end to the other showing a part of your body lifted high.

TASK 4—Grasping the pole, can you get from one side of the pole to the other with a part of your body lifted high?

MATS AND CANES

TASK 1—Jump over the cane with your head high and travel over the mat with another part high.

TASK 2—Roll over the mat with either your seat or toes high.

TASK 3—Canes at different heights. Travel over one cane with one part of your body high and over another cane with a different part high.

Movement Training

WHOLE BODY

TASK 1—Move from one part of your body to another keeping your feet together. How many different parts of your body can you use?

TASK 2—Move from one part of your body to another keeping your feet apart. How many different parts of your body can you use?

TASK 3—Move from one part of your body to another sometimes with your feet together and sometimes with feet apart.

Weight supported on the arms

TASK 1—Keeping your hands on the floor, make patterns round them with your feet sometimes having them close together and sometimes far apart.

TASK 2—Move about the floor on your hands and feet in different ways keeping your feet close together.

TASK 3—Move about the floor on your hands and feet in different ways keeping your feet far apart.

TASK 4—Move about the floor in different ways bringing your feet together and then parting them.

TASK 5—Put your hands on the floor and lift or jump your feet in the air. Can you bring your feet down one after the other?

TASK 6—Put your hands on the floor and lift or jump your feet in the air. Can you land with your feet close together?

TASK 7—Put your hands on the floor and lift or jump your feet in the air. Keep your feet close together all the time. (Keep your head up.)

TASK 8—Put your hands on the floor, lift or jump your feet in the air trying to part them. (Keep your head up.)

Leg work

TASK 1—Jump (a) on the spot (b) travelling, keeping your feet close together in the air.

TASK 2—Jump on the spot. Find different ways of parting your feet in the air.

TASK 3—Run and jump bringing your feet close together in the air.

TASK 4—Run and jump parting your feet in the air.

TASK 5—Run and jump. Find the different ways in which you can have your feet together in the air. (e.g. the feet can be together with both legs stretched or both legs bent, in front, behind or to the side.)

TASK 6—Run and jump. Find different ways of having the feet apart in the air. (e.g. one leg can be forward and one back; the legs can be stretched sideways or one leg can be stretched and one can be bent, etc.)

Apparatus

LONDON APPARATUS

TASK 1—Travel on the apparatus keeping your feet together.

TASK 2—Travel on the apparatus keeping your feet apart.

TASK 3—Travel on the apparatus first with your feet together and then with your feet apart.

ESSEX APPARATUS

TASK 1—Travel up a plank by parting your feet; jump off the stool keeping your feet together.

TASK 2—Travel across a plank with your feet close together or far apart.

MATS AND CANES

TASK 1—Jump over the cane with your feet apart, then roll over the mat with your feet together.

TASK 2—With your hands on the ground travel over a low cane and then over a mat with your feet either close together or wide apart.

TASK 3—Travel over the cane with your feet together and over the mat with your feet apart.

III. MOVING WITH HANDS NEAR TO THE FEET OR AWAY FROM THE FEET

Movement Training

WHOLE BODY

TASK 1—Move in different ways with your feet near to your hands.

TASK 2—Move in different ways with your feet far away from your hands.

TASK 3—Move in different ways sometimes with your feet near to your hands and sometimes with your feet far away from your hands.

WEIGHT SUPPORTED ON THE ARMS

TASK 1—With only your hands and feet touching the floor move about keeping them near to each other.

TASK 2—With only your hands and feet touching the floor move about keeping them far from each other.

TASK 3—Put your hands on the floor and pushing hard to lift feet, can you get them far away from your hands while they are in the air? Bring your feet down very softly.

LEG WORK

TASK 1—Run and jump. Choose a position in the air with your hands touching your feet. How many other positions can you find? (Keep your head up.)

TASK 2—Run and jump. Stretch so that your feet are far away from your hands while you are in the air. How many different ways can you do this?

Apparatus

LONDON APPARATUS

TASK 1—Travel on the apparatus with your hands and feet near to each other.

TASK 2—Travel on the apparatus with your hands and feet far apart.

TASK 3—Travel on the apparatus sometimes with your hands and feet near to each other and sometimes with them far apart.

ESSEX APPARATUS

TASK 1—Travel up a plank with your hands and feet near to each other. Come off the stool with them as far apart as possible.

TASK 2—Travel along a pole sometimes with your hands and feet near each other and sometimes with them far apart.

MATS AND CANES

TASK 1—Travel under or over canes with either your hands or feet near to each other or with them far apart.

IV. CURLING AND STRETCHING

Movement Training

WHOLE BODY

TASK 1—Curl up. Which part of you is touching the floor? Find another part to support you and curl up again. Find many different parts on which you can be curled.

TASK 2—As above, but stretching out instead of curling up.

TASK 3—Curl up on one part of your body and then stretch out. Repeat on different parts of your body.

TASK 4—Move with your body curled up.

TASK 5—Move with your body stretched out.

TASK 6—Move about the room changing continuously from being curled up to being stretched out.

WEIGHT SUPPORTED ON THE ARMS

TASK 1—Move in different ways on your hands and feet with your body curled up.

TASK 2—Move in different ways on your hands and feet with your body stretched out.

TASK 3—Put your hands on the floor (keep your head up). Try to lift your feet off the floor keeping your body curled.

TASK 4—As above, with your body stretched.

LEG WORK

(As a safety precaution the children should be reminded to keep their heads up in the following tasks and therefore the body will not in fact be curled.)

TASK 1—Travel with only your feet touching the floor, keeping low so that your legs are bent. You can move with both feet together or one after the other.

TASK 2—Travel with only your feet touching the floor, stretching your legs as you move.

TASK 3—Travel with only your feet touching the floor, sometimes with your legs bent and sometimes with them stretched.

TASK 4—Run and leap and show a curled position in the air.

TASK 5—As above showing a stretched position in the air.

Apparatus

LONDON APPARATUS

TASK 1—Find different places on the apparatus where you can hold on in a curled position.

TASK 2—Find different places on the apparatus where you can hold on in a stretched position.

TASK 3—Find different places on the apparatus where you can curl and stretch.

TASK 4—Travel on the apparatus curling and stretching as you move.

ESSEX APPARATUS

TASK 1—Travel up the plank on to the stool with your body curled, come off the stool with your body stretched. (See note on page 28, Essex Apparatus, Task 1.)

TASK 2—Find ways of moving from one side of the pole to the other. Can you make your body curl or stretch as you travel?

TASK 3—Find ways of travelling between the poles (at the frame), curling and/or stretching as you move.

CANES AND MATS

TASK 1—Taking your weight on your hands travel over a cane, stretching your body—then roll over the mat curling your body.

TASK 2—Travel over or under the canes either curling or stretching. (Canes can be either on the floor or raised at different heights.)

TASK 3—Run and jump over the first cane showing a curled position in the air, and over the second cane showing a stretched position in the air.

V. TWISTING AND TURNING

Movement Training

WHOLE BODY

TASK 1—Keeping one part of your body still on the floor, twist the rest of your body as far as you can. Keep changing the part of your body which is on the floor and find how many different ways you can twist.

33

Task 2—Travel, twisting from one part of your body to another.

WEIGHT SUPPORTED ON THE ARMS

Task 1—Move on your hands and feet twisting as you travel about the floor.

Task 2—Twist to put your hands on the floor to one side of your feet. Jump your feet or seat into the air bringing your feet down near your hands.

LEG WORK

Task 1—Jump, twisting or turning in the air. (Later, run and jump.)

Task 2—Run and jump, make a twisted shape in the air with your body.

Apparatus

LONDON APPARATUS

Task 1—Find different places on the apparatus where you can grip with your hands and feet. Can you twist the rest of your body?

Task 2—Using your hands and feet twist and turn as you travel on the apparatus.

Task 3—Find different places on the apparatus where you can make a twisted shape, gripping with your hands and any other part of your body.

Task 4—Using your hands and any other part of your body twist and turn as you travel on the apparatus.

ESSEX APPARATUS

Task 1—Travel up one plank without twisting and come down the other using a twist.

Task 2—Travel up the plank in different ways, come off the stool with a twist.

Task 3—Travel from one pole to the other (on the frame) with a twist.

MATS AND CANES

Task 1—Run and jump over the cane twisting in the air.

Task 2—Travel over the cane and then the mat, showing one movement with a twist and one without.

VI. SHAPE

The body can hold or move through certain shapes. These are the long narrow extended shape, the wide sideways extended and the compact rounded shapes; children also enjoy holding a twisted shape.

Movement Training

WHOLE BODY

TASK 1—Make a rounded shape with your body. Which part of your body is on the floor? Can you put another part of your body on the floor and make a rounded shape again? How many ways can you find?

TASK 2—As above making a wide shape.

TASK 3—As above making a long extended shape.

TASK 4—As above making a twisted shape.

TASK 5—Starting from a rounded shape stretch or twist your body to make another shape.

TASK 6—Travel about the floor and as you move make one shape with your body and then change and make a different one.

WEIGHT SUPPORTED ON THE ARMS

TASK 1—Move in different ways on your hands and feet showing a wide shape. (This can be repeated with any of the other shapes.)

TASK 2—Put your hands on the floor (keep your head up). Try to lift your feet off the floor showing a round shape. (This can be repeated with any of the other shapes.)

LEG WORK

TASK 1—From standing, jump showing (*a*) a wide shape or (*b*) a long thin shape or (*c*) a rounded shape or (*d*) a twisted shape, while you are in the air.

TASK 2—Run and jump showing shapes as in task 1. (Guide the children to discover which is the appropriate take-off for their jump—one or two feet.)

C*

Apparatus

LONDON APPARATUS

TASK 1—Find different places on the apparatus where you can make one shape, i.e. narrow extended, wide sideways, compact rounded or twisted shape.

TASK 2—Travel on the apparatus with your body in one shape.

TASK 3—Travel on the apparatus changing from one shape to another.

ESSEX APPARATUS

TASK 1—Travel up one plank making one shape and down the other making a different shape.

TASK 2—Travel across a pole or plank making a long (or some other) shape.

TASK 3—Run to a stool and arrive on it in a rounded shape. Come down the plank making a long shape.

MATS AND CANES

TASK 1—Travel over two canes showing a different shape over each one.

TASK 2—Travel over or under cane showing a long shape and over the mat showing a rounded shape.

CHAPTER III

THE OUTDOOR LESSON

It should be recognized that the outdoor facilities offer a different setting for physical education and that the lesson should not be a diluted form of the agility lesson taken in the hall.

In the playground the children have the advantage of working in the fresh air and although there are times when the weather is unsuitable for work outside, whenever possible the outdoor lesson should be included in the programme of activity. The greater space of the playground, with its lack of encumbrances, gives opportunities for the children to enjoy and pursue with purpose activities such as bowling a hoop, running and jumping, etc. The learning of these skills, where space is an essential factor, is not often possible in a hall. On the other hand, the cold dirty surface of a playground is not suitable for experimentation in the transference of weight.

The good habit of stripping should be continued for the playground lesson. The children need plimsolls and a woollen jersey should be worn when the weather is cool.

An adequate supply of small apparatus is essential for an effective lesson. This should include a hoop, a skipping rope, a bat and a small ball for each child. The most suitable ball for use with a bat is a perforated plastic one. In addition there should be a number of large balls (minimum 10), beanbags, canes, skittles or similar supports. All the apparatus should be stored in suitable containers so that it may be spread out in the playground enabling every child to obtain apparatus speedily and without fuss.

Some playground marking, including marks on walls for target practice, is valuable. These should be planned with care, however, as unnecessary lines or a lack of lines both create difficulties. Although the outdoor lesson will be one in which the children use small apparatus and practise a variety of skills, it will vary in form according to the apparatus used.

EARLY STAGES

Here, as in the agility lesson, emphasis is placed on establishing response and confidence. In order to achieve these the children should be trained to listen to simple instructions, to space well and to move freely with the small apparatus. It may be necessary to limit the area of play in the case of difficult, irregular-shaped playgrounds as the teacher should be able to see all the class. It is essential, at this stage, that the children are trained to look after the apparatus. This applies to general use, distribution and collection. Time should be left at the end of a lesson to look for balls which seem to be lost.

The lesson may start with a free choice of apparatus and proceed to all working with one type; or it may start with all the children working with one type of apparatus and end with a choice. The main purpose of the lesson is to help the children in the general handling of the various pieces of apparatus. Some teaching of a simple technique may be given as the need arises.

SUGGESTIONS OF ACTIVITIES

1.   Go to the nearest apparatus box, take a piece of apparatus and play with it. Keep moving. (Encourage the children to find different ways of playing with the apparatus. They should be trained to put one piece of apparatus away before taking a different piece.)

2.   Find two different ways of playing with your apparatus.

3.   Go to the box and take a ball; play with your ball. Keep moving.

4.   Play with your ball keeping it (i) on or near the ground, (ii) up in the air.

5.   Throw the ball in the air, let it bounce and catch it. (Teach the technique of catching.)

6.   Take a hoop, play with it, keep moving. (Train the children to keep level with the hoop when bowling to avoid collisions.)

7.   Find two different movements that you can do with your hoop using your hands.

8.   Put your hoop on the ground. Lift it up, carry it to a new place and put it down quietly. Find different ways of going in

and out of your hoop. (The children should avoid putting hands and bodies on the ground as the playground surface is unsuitable.)

9. With your hoop on the ground, show different ways of going over it.

10. With your hoop on the ground, show different ways of going round it.

In the early stages a lesson may be composed of one or more of the above activities.

PROGRESSION FROM THE EARLY STAGES

Now the lesson will take a more definite form and be planned on similar lines to the agility lesson. The order will be:

> Opening Activity.
> Skill Training.
> Climax.

with the skill training as a preparation for the climax. Lessons will vary according to the type of apparatus used and activity pursued but in the main they can be divided as follows:

I. The emphasis may be on running or jumping using one or several types of obstacle; or one piece of apparatus, such as a hoop or rope only may be used and a variety of skills developed with it.

II. A whole lesson may be devoted to the use of balls or bats and balls and appropriate skills developed. The children will work individually before progressing to working with a partner or in a small group.

III. A lesson consisting mainly of group practices may be taken with the older children. Some of the activities will have been previously introduced to the whole class. Sometimes it is helpful to take a lesson of this type when apparatus, such as large balls, is in short supply or a wall space which is needed for a particular practice, is limited.

DEVELOPMENT OF SKILLS

Material for the lesson should be planned in advance. The children will use the apparatus experimentally and much can be done to help the natural development of the skills during this time. However, the teacher should have thought out the basic skills which need to be encouraged and, if they do not develop, she should devise situations which will guide the children to discover these skills for themselves. Once the basic skills are known, she can then set tasks which stimulate the children to produce variety in their work by the added use of Space and Time, e.g. changes of level, direction and speed. The skills listed below are intended for the teacher's reference and not as set exercises.

The work is concerned with the handling of apparatus and skilful footwork in order to develop the co-ordination of hands, eyes and feet. After teaching the simple handling of hoops, ropes and balls, the aim should be to encourage the children to develop the ability to run or jump whilst controlling the apparatus.

SKILLS WITHOUT APPARATUS

Good running and jumping are dependent upon good footwork and from an early stage footwork practices should be given to build up mobility, strength and co-ordination. In order to jump well the children need strong legs and to be able to propel themselves into the air. Variety in jumping should be encouraged: this will include jumping for height, for length, with a change of direction, or from a stationary position.

1. Run making patterns with the feet.
2. Dodge, making the feet move quickly and lightly in different directions.
3. Run quickly to a given spot and stop quite still.
4. Run and on a signal change direction.
5. Run continuously at the same speed trying to get an easy rhythmical action.
6. Run and change speed while travelling in the same direction.
7. Run and change speed and direction.

8. Run quickly and gradually decrease speed.
9. Run slowly and gradually increase speed.
10. Run and jump and continue to run and jump.
11. Run and jump and try to stop on landing.
12. Run and jump turning to land in a different direction and continue to run in the changed direction.
13. Run and jump high in the air with the feet together.
14. Run and jump high in the air with the feet apart.
15. Jump for length from a standing position.
16. Jump from two feet on to two feet continuously.

SKILLS WITH APPARATUS

HOOPS
1. Free play.
2. Bowl. Show the children how to place one hand on top to steady the hoop and the use of the other hand flat to bat the hoop forward.
3. Spin a hoop.
4. Swing a hoop backwards and forwards and jump in and out as it swings.
5. Skip with a hoop (i) on the spot, (ii) travelling, (iii) with a change of direction and (iv) with a change of speed.
6. Bowl a hoop and run round in front of it.
7. Spin a hoop and run round quickly.
8. Jump over a small hoop as it bowls along.
9. Jump over a spinning hoop.
10. Jump in, out or over a hoop.
11. Find different ways of moving round a hoop on the ground.
12. Dodge and run in and out of a series of hoops on the ground.
13. Run and jump into a hoop held by a partner.
14. Run and jump over hoops for length or height.

ROPES
1. Using individual ropes on the ground practise jumping for length.
2. Find different ways of skipping.
3. Skip on the spot.

4. Skip travelling.
5. Skip with the feet together.
6. Skip from one foot to the other.
7. Make up a pattern when skipping and repeat it.

All skipping activities can be performed with the rope turning forward or backward at different speeds with or without a rebound, and with the feet travelling in different directions. Once they are competent the children should be encouraged to increase the number of times that they can skip continuously using any one of these ways.

CANES

1. A cane each, on the ground, run and jump over it. Find different ways of jumping from one foot and two feet and also with a turn.

2. A cane raised off the ground either held by a partner or supported on skittles, jumping stands, blocks, tins, etc. Run and jump the cane. Try to jump sideways as well as forwards. (The children should work in couples or, where space is limited, in small groups of not more than four.)

Safety Precaution—Any raised canes, hoops or ropes must be free to fall if touched.

BALLS

The aim should be to develop co-ordination and skill in handling balls and bats. The children should be trained to use their eyes to watch a moving object and to meet the many changing situations such as speed, direction and strength, all of which occur in a game. A player is rarely static, and for this reason once a technique has been learned it should be practised on the move and used in a variety of ways.

Skills should be developed in the following ways:

1. Free play with balls and bats/balls. The child becomes familiar with the apparatus and learns much during this time.

2. Teach the skill slowly, emphasising the important points. Time should be given later for the practice of the skill on the move, either walking or running.

3. When the skill is learned, encourage the child to use it in a variety of ways and then with changes of time, changes of

42

direction, using either hand or either foot, strongly or lightly. This should help to develop adaptability to varying situations.

4. The children should be encouraged to create records in the number of times they can repeat an action continuously.

5. Some older children may be ready to use the skill in co-operation with a partner and later in a small group.

Use of balls and development of skills

I. Dribbling

Dribble the ball (*a*) with the foot.
　　　　　　　(*b*) with the bat.

In dribbling, the aim is to keep close to the ball which is propelled along the ground by light continuous tapping.

SUGGESTIONS FOR VARIETY IN THE USE OF THE SKILL

WORKING INDIVIDUALLY

Dribble the ball:—1. walking and running.
　　　　　　　　　2. with changes of direction.
　　　　　　　　　3. with changes of speed.
　　　　　　　　　4. weaving in and out of obstacles.
　　　　　　　　　5. moving along a straight line.
　　　　　　　　　6. moving from a starting line to a mark and back again.
　　　　　　　　　7. hitting or kicking; aim into a space or at a wall.

WORKING IN PAIRS

1. Standing on opposite sides of the playground, dribble the ball to a partner who dribbles it back.

2. Dribble with the feet trying to keep the ball away from an opponent.

3. Travel round the playground, dribbling and passing in pairs.

4. Dribble and kick the ball through a gap (made with bean-bags) to a partner; gradually make the gap narrower.

WORKING IN GROUPS

1. Each child with a ball dribbles it freely and speedily—three or four ' pirates ' without balls watch for loose ones, trap

them and continue dribbling. Those left without balls become ' pirates '.

2. Small groups each with a large ball, travel round the playground dribbling and kicking from one to another using everyone in the group.

II. Rolling and Fielding

To train good rolling of the ball, the children should be encouraged to make a full swing of the arm with the feet in opposition. In fielding, they should go to meet the ball (hands together, palms towards the ball, fingers pointing down), reaching out to collect and gather it in.

SUGGESTIONS FOR VARIETY IN THE USE OF THE SKILL

WORKING INDIVIDUALLY

1. Roll the ball, run after it and field it.
2. Roll the ball, jump over it and field it.
3. Roll the ball against a wall and field it.
4. Roll the ball at a skittle or a beanbag from a distance of at least 10 feet.

WORKING IN PAIRS

1. Standing approximately 10 yards apart, roll the ball to a partner who fields it and rolls it back.
2. Rolling the ball into a space for a partner to chase and field.
3. Repeat individual activities 3 and 4 above, working with a partner.

III. Bouncing and Catching

When learning the skill of bouncing a ball, the children can also practise catching it. They should be encouraged to reach for it and gather it in with relaxed hands.

SUGGESTIONS FOR VARIETY IN THE USE OF THE SKILL

WORKING INDIVIDUALLY

1. Throw the ball in the air, let it bounce then catch it.
2. Bounce and catch the ball using different degrees of strength—low and high bounces. (For a strong, high, bounce use should be made of the whole body and the feet should be in opposition.)

44

3.   Bounce the ball against a wall and catch.

   1.   Bounce and catch the ball.
   2.   Bounce the ball into a hoop to a partner. Later repeat moving round the hoop.
   3.   Bounce the ball against a wall. The partner should try to catch it.

WORKING IN GROUPS
   1.   In groups of three or four, bouncing and catching on the move.

IV. Throwing and Catching

   (a) *Underarm throwing*—The action is similar to that of rolling with the emphasis on the swing of the arm as the weight is transferred from the back to the front foot. The latter should be in opposition to the arm used.

   (b) *Overarm throwing*—For this skill the essential points to train are the ' sideways on ' position, the opposition of the throwing arm and the forward foot, and the thrust forward in the follow through as the weight is transferred from the back to the front foot.

SUGGESTIONS FOR VARIETY IN THE USE OF THE SKILL

WORKING INDIVIDUALLY
   1.   Throwing underarm into a space, run to pick up the ball.
   2.   Throwing overarm into a space, run to pick up the ball.
   3.   Throw underarm/overarm against a wall, catch the ball as it rebounds.
   4.   As 3, aiming at a target.

WORKING IN PAIRS
   The above skills 1—4 can be taken with a partner.

WORKING IN GROUPS
   1.   In small groups keep a large ball moving with under or overarm throwing. Keep your feet as well as the ball moving.
   2.   As 1, travelling across the playground.
   3.   As 1, with one ' pirate ' who tries to get the ball.

V. **Batting**

In this skill the hand or bat can be used. Pat-bouncing downwards, upwards, round the body and on the move can be followed by hitting the ball forwards. In hitting the ball forwards with hand or bat, encourage the ' sideways on ' position and the full swing of the arm.

WORKING INDIVIDUALLY
1. Bat downwards. (Pat-bouncing with the hand.)
2. Bat upwards, allowing a bounce if necessary.
3. Bat alternately downwards and upwards.
4. Bat using one hand only or alternate hands.
5. Bouncing the ball at the side, bat it into a space or against a wall.
6. Bat continuously against a wall.

WORKING IN PAIRS
1. Pat-bounce with a partner.
2. Bat in pairs against a wall.
3. Bat over a cane or rope. (Net.)
4. Bat the ball thrown or bounced by a partner.

EXAMPLES OF LESSONS

LESSON FOR A FIVE YEAR OLD CLASS

1. OPENING ACTIVITY
   (i) Free play with small apparatus. (Individual help by the teacher.)
   (ii) Put the apparatus away, all take a ball and play freely.

2. SKILL TRAINING
   (i) Play with your ball keeping it (*a*) on or near the ground, (*b*) up in the air.
   (ii) Roll the ball into a space, run after it and stop it.

3. CLIMAX
   (i) Free play with apparatus again, balls can be changed for a different piece of apparatus.

(ii) Apparatus away, walk round and check the apparatus in the corners.

LESSON FOR A SIX YEAR OLD CLASS. (Hoops)

1. OPENING ACTIVITY
   (i) A hoop each, free play.
   (ii) Hoops on the ground, run round as many as you can without touching them.
2. SKILL TRAINING
   (i) Bowling the hoop freely about the playground.
   (ii) Spin the hoop and run round it as many times as you can before it falls.
3. CLIMAX
   In pairs, one hoop between two. Keep the hoop moving.

LESSON FOR A SIX YEAR OLD CLASS. (Balls)

1. OPENING ACTIVITY
   Free play with any piece of small apparatus.
2. SKILL TRAINING
   (i) Throw the ball up, let it bounce then catch it. Keep moving.
   (ii) Bounce the ball as hard as possible on the spot, move to catch it.
3. CLIMAX
   (i) Bounce the ball against a wall, partner moves to catch it and repeats.
   (ii) Bounce and catch to a partner on the move.

LESSON FOR A SEVEN YEAR OLD CLASS. (Ropes)

1. OPENING ACTIVITY
   Free play with any apparatus.
2. SKILL TRAINING
   (i) Skip freely with a rope. (The teacher should give help to those unable to skip.)
   (ii) Skip—(a) travelling, (b) on the spot.
   (iii) Rope on the ground, jump for distance.
3. CLIMAX
   Groups of three with one rope. Make up a game using any of the above skills.

47

LESSON FOR A SEVEN YEAR OLD CLASS. (Balls)

1. OPENING ACTIVITY
   Free play with any piece of apparatus.

2. SKILL TRAINING
     (i) Run, bounce ball well ahead and catch it.
    (ii) In two's, accurate under and overarm throw to a partner at a reasonable distance.
   (iii) Repeat (ii), moving.

3. CLIMAX
   Large balls groups of four or five children who aim to ' keep the ball moving '.
   Make the skill more challenging by giving the children the aim of catching the ball continuously for a set number of times. Each group should aim to finish first.

LESSON FOR A SEVEN YEAR OLD CLASS. (Composite lesson)

1. OPENING ACTIVITY
   Free play with a ball.

2. SKILL TRAINING
   Free practice of batting the ball with bat or hand: do this in different directions and at different speeds.

3. CLIMAX
   Working in four groups.
     (i) With small balls and bats, work individually batting against a wall.
    (ii) Three or four children jump supported cane.
   (iii) In groups of three or four keep a large ball moving with one ' pirate '.
    (iv) Skip individually or with a partner or in a group.

CHAPTER IV

DANCE

Many teachers in Infant schools make good use of the weekly B.B.C. Music and Movement lessons and the children derive great enjoyment and value from them. The programme covers both music and movement and the basic principles of the movement training are the same as advocated in this book. The B.B.C. issues notes on the work in their programme which are intended to give help to the teacher. Full use should be made of these because the work varies from class to class and often it is helpful if part or all of the lesson is followed up at a later stage in the week.

Many teachers will wish to take their own dance lesson and for these, the following notes and suggestions are given.

From the earliest age children express their desires and frustrations through movement. After they are able to balance and walk, they progress to ' prancing ' and readily give relief to their immediate feelings by this form of expressive movement. At this stage no outside stimulus is necessary as the movement is spontaneous and is often the result of the imagination. In teaching dance this spontaneous and imaginative movement must be fostered and later directed by the teacher, providing situations for this outlet. The teacher aims at developing the whole child through encouraging the use of movement and imagination to express and communicate ideas and moods. Dance takes its place with art, music and drama and is useful in integrating these arts.

The aims of dance may be listed as follows:

1. To train the children in another creative art form.

2. To awaken and preserve the children's impulses and spontaneity.

3. To develop poise and confidence.

4. To train the control of the body and an understanding of its powers and limitations.

5. To train intelligent listening to accompaniment.

6. To train co-operation with others in creative work.

D

EARLY STAGES

Very young children dance spontaneously to the accompaniment of music or percussion and opportunity should be given for this. The children will tend to run and ' twirl ' unless it is suggested by the teacher that they try other things with their feet, for example skip, hop, jump, gallop, etc. In the main the movement is limited to the legs and the arms and little or no use is made of the body. It will be necessary, therefore, to make the child aware of the part(s) of the body so that the ' whole child ' may participate in the dance. In order to foster this ' Body Awareness ' the children may be asked to dance with their knees, elbows or chest and to discover what they can do with the whole body, for example, folding up and opening out. Further experience will be gained by the children dancing low, near the floor and then high, near the ceiling, or by moving quickly and slowly. The use of simple phrasing will develop this free movement into a dance form. An easy way of introducing this is by the teacher giving a rhythm for the children's movement of ' travel and stop ', using her voice or percussion as the stimulus.

A list of suggested activities, which the teacher may use to supplement her own ideas, follows. They are mainly concerned with Body Awareness and how the various parts of the body can be used in dance. Further variety is encouraged by the use of levels, time and phrasing.

Feet

1. Travel from one spot to another and stop. The teacher uses her voice or percussion to indicate the start and finish. (Phrasing.)

2. Repeat 1, the children making their own phrases.

3. Travel from one spot to another starting low and finishing high.

4. Travel and spin on the spot.

5. Travel and spin on the spot finishing high or low.

6. Travel from one spot to another using the feet in different ways. (Long steps, small steps, skips, hops, jumps, heels and toes, etc.).

7. Run and leap. Repeat, introducing phrasing as soon as possible.

Hands

1. Look at your hands. Shake them. What other movements can you do with them? E.g. clapping, beating the floor, rubbing together, closing and opening out, squeezing and shaking.
2. Repeat any of the movements in 1, introducing a simple rhythm.
3. Repeat 2, working at different levels.
4. Make a shape with one hand, now with the other hand. Can you make your hands ' talk '? (Question and answer.)
5. One hand leading the other, make a pattern round your body.
6. Move your hands close to your body, then far away from your body.

Hands and Feet

1. Travel to a spot dancing with your feet; on the spot dance with your hands.
2. Travel to a spot dancing with your hands and feet.

The suggestions under the separate headings of ' Feet ' and ' Hands ' can be combined in various ways, e.g. Dance to a spot finishing low, beating the floor with your hands or finishing high, clapping your hands.

Whole Body

1. Close yourself up as small as you can, open out as big as you can.
2. Repeat trying to open out at different levels.
3. Close up quickly/slowly and open out slowly/quickly. Develop a rhythm.
4. Repeat 3, travelling.

In order to make the children aware of parts of the body, other than their feet and hands, they may be asked to dance with their chest, hip, shoulder, elbow, knee, etc.

It is important to remember that dance is concerned with the expressive side of movement and in order to foster this the children should be encouraged to feel ' HOW ' they move. Before this quality can be developed attention should be directed towards Body Awareness (the ' WHAT ' of movement).

D*

THE ANALYSIS OF MOVEMENT WITH REFERENCE TO DANCE

Body Awareness. (WHAT the body is doing.)

In this, concentration should be centred on the awareness of the whole body or part(s) of the body in movement.

E.g. 1. The body can bend, stretch and twist.
2. Different parts of the body can meet and part.
3. Emphasis can be laid on one half of the body, e.g. the lower part (hips and legs), which may be used for locomotion and elevation; the upper part (arms, chest and head), which may be used for gestures, etc.
4. Part of the body can initiate a movement.
5. The body can travel on different parts.

Body Awareness is an essential part of the development of dance and therefore every lesson should include some work on this important aspect before the expressive side is attempted.

Time. (HOW the body is moving.)

The quality of time is expressed in dance by either a feeling of (*a*) suddenness or (*b*) sustainment. This is shown in (*a*) by a hurried excited movement where there is a feeling of leaping ahead and in (*b*) by a lingering where the children enjoy the time taken to perform the movement. Phrasing and rhythmic form should be introduced after a short period of exploration.

Weight. (HOW the body is moving.)

Weight is the term used to indicate a degree of muscular tension in the body. Where there is little tension lightness is felt, where there is much tension, strength is felt. The focal point of light movement is the breast bone and that of strong movement the abdomen. The arms play an important part in light movement and therefore the stress is usually in an upward direction, whereas the legs are important in strong movement and therefore the stress is usually in the downward direction.

Space. (HOW the body is moving.)

The quality of space is concerned with directness or flexibility of movement. Direct movement is any action which travels along a path without deviations. Flexible movement involves continuous changes of the direction of a movement using a roundabout or twisted path.

Flow. (HOW the body is moving.)

The flow of movement can be either bound or free. It is termed ' bound ' when the action can be stopped or held at any point in the movement or ' free ' when there is abandonment or lack of control and the movement is difficult to stop.

Space. (WHERE the body is going.)

In addition to the quality of space there are other aspects of space which play an increasingly large part in dance. These are concerned with where the body or parts of the body move in space, e.g.:
  (1) extensions—near to and far from the body.
  (2) level   —high, medium and low.
  (3) direction —forwards, backwards, sideways, upwards and downwards.
  (4) path   —floor and space patterns.
All of these make an important contribution to dance composition.

In working on these movement qualities it will be found that the children can more easily feel and express the appropriate movement by experimenting in the use of the two extremes of the quality. It is essential that these qualities are experienced in conjunction with body awareness (WHAT).
E.g. ' Dance with your feet strongly and then lightly '; rather than ' Dance strongly and lightly '.

PROGRESSION FROM THE EARLY STAGES

PLANNING A LESSON

Before taking any dance session it is essential for the teacher to prepare and write down the proposed lesson. It is comparatively simple to find a suitable movement idea for Infant dance, but the development of this idea may present problems. The plan for the lesson should include training in body awareness, space awareness and the quality of movement and the work covered in the first part should be a preparation for the climax. When preparing a lesson or a series of lessons the following plan may prove to be a useful guide.

Opening. A simple movement probably involving travelling and the use of the general space.

Movement Training. To include work on body awareness, space and quality.

Climax. 1. Dramatic form
     or 2. A simple dance study
     or 3. Interpretation of suitable pieces of music.

Some suggestions of movement ideas are given and tasks framed on the first of these ideas also follow. Once the children are aware of dancing with the whole of their bodies to express the movement idea as well as using the available space sensibly, the experience can be developed into whichever of the three possibilities of the climax of the lesson the teacher wishes to pursue.

SOME MOVEMENT IDEAS

1. Strong and light.
2. Opening and closing.
3. Flexible and direct.
4. Spiky and smooth.
5. Levels.
6. Going and stopping, and travelling continuously.
7. Sudden and sustained.
8. Size of movement. (See page 61.)

DEVELOPMENT OF THE MOVEMENT IDEA OF STRONG AND LIGHT

Movement Training

    1. Look at your hands, make them strong in as many ways as you can.

    2. Choose one way and move your hands strongly, e.g. punching, pushing, slashing, wringing, etc.

3. Develop one of the above to a definite rhythm.

4. Make your hands light in different ways. Develop this as in 1—3 above.

5. Move, using your legs strongly.

6. Take your weight on different parts and still use your legs strongly.

7. Travel stamping and pressing with your feet. Develop this to a rhythm.

8. Move using your legs lightly. Develop this as in 5—7.

9. Choose another part of your body and use it strongly/lightly, e.g. shoulder, elbow, hips, etc.

10. On the spot or travelling, move using the whole body strongly/lightly.

11. Alternating strong and light movements, dance to a definite rhythm.

12. Run and leap high in the air.

13. Find other ways of using your legs strongly to lift you high in the air, e.g. skipping, galloping, etc.

14. Punch low towards the floor, punch high towards the ceiling. Develop a rhythm.

15. With light movements travel near the floor and then far away from the floor. Repeat using strong movements.

16. With strong movements travel near the floor and with light movements travel high in the air.

17. Travel to a spot finishing in a strong shape near the floor; repeat finishing in a light shape at a high level.

Climax or Development

1. DRAMATIC FORM

When thinking of a suitable climax to a dance lesson, it is important that the teacher keeps in mind the quality she has been training in the first part of the lesson. Too often this quality is lost both in the minds of the teacher and children because of the strong appeal of the dramatic idea or story. It may help the teacher to choose one of the following ideas to develop the experience of strength and lightness gained in the earlier part of the lesson.

1. The sea.

2. Seasons.

3. Toy shop.
4. Fireworks.
5. Puppets.
6. Circus.
7. Red Indians.
8. Simple stories.

A dramatic dance based on the idea of autumn could depict the wind blowing strongly to scatter the leaves from the tops of the trees (high level) to the ground (low level). They could whirl and flutter lightly in the air and finally settle on the ground. Then they could be brushed up strongly by the sweepers.

2. SIMPLE DANCE STUDY

A simple dance could be developed by the children working in pairs on a ' question and answer ' idea, one child ' speaking ' with strong movements and the other ' replying ' with light movements. The children might also work in two groups of boys and girls, the girls expressing the light quality and the boys expressing the strong quality. The girls could move freely in the hall and then respond to the boys' strong movements which ' drive ' them to the centre.

3. INTERPRETATION OF A SUITABLE PIECE OF MUSIC

For this, the teacher must first select a suitable piece of music which will stimulate the children to move using the qualities worked on in the first part of the lesson. It is important that the piece of music is short so that it can be repeated several times, the children beginning to recognize and know the different parts. They should first sit and listen to it and when it is repeated they might move their hands to interpret the music. They could then get up and dance to it. It is here that the teacher must use her powers of observation and be prepared to give the necessary help in interpreting the music in order to eliminate mere ' prancing '. Simple questions could be put to the children to guide them in their listening such as: When does the music tell you to go and stop? Listen to it telling you to dance strongly. Where does it tell you to twist, turn and swirl?

Other movement ideas (page 54) can be developed in a similar way to the example given (Strong and Light). The movement

training section should include tasks based on the chosen movement idea and these should be developed in one of the three
possible ways suggested to form the climax of the lesson.

As well as using the list of ideas on page 56, teachers will be
able to draw on their wide experience of suitable topics for their
classes and possibly link their dance lesson with some project
which is being followed in the classroom. As the work develops,
it will be found that more than one movement idea can be used
in a lesson. For example, in a lesson based on level of movement,
the quality of time can be stressed as well, so widening the
children's experience.

PARTNER AND GROUP WORK

Children in the Infants' school are characterized by their
individuality. It is important that they are given the opportunity
to express themselves in their own way and therefore most of
their experience will be gained by dancing on their own. However,
this does not preclude the teacher from introducing partner and
simple group movements as the work develops. One obvious
advantage is that the children learn to work with other children.
When working with a partner or in a group, the relationship may
be in one of the following forms.

1. MEETING AND PARTING

Using the movement idea of the lesson, the children dance to
meet their partners and dance away from them. Progression can
be made by the children dancing round and/or with their partners
before parting.

2. 'CONVERSATION'

Facing one another, the children converse in movement. They
may 'talk' together with the same type of movement or move
alternately with the same or contrasting type of movement.

3. LEADING AND FOLLOWING

One child dances to a new place and stops; she is then followed
by her partner. They can dance using the movement idea of the
lesson with similar or contrasting movements.

4. STATUES

The sequence of movement in 3 can be repeated and the emphasis placed on the ' stopping '. The child can express the chosen movement idea in the form of a statue, e.g. a spiky shape, a high level, etc.

ACCOMPANIMENT

It is important to introduce some form of accompaniment from the earliest stage; although it need not be used throughout the lesson it aids the ' feel ' of the movement and helps the children to recognize rhythm and phrasing.

With most children leaping and running change naturally from the athletic movement to dance when performed to accompaniment. The form this may take is varied. The teacher herself may either accompany with her voice, percussion or a piano. Records and tape recordings may also be used. At a later stage the children may accompany themselves with various pieces of percussion or with their voices.

Accompaniment by the teacher

If a teacher accompanies her class on the piano, she should be sufficiently skilled to play music that will stimulate the type of movement she hopes to obtain from the children. It is also necessary for her to observe her class and give appropriate guidance. It may be more valuable therefore, if she plays for part of the lesson only, for example the climax, and uses a percussion instrument for the remainder of the lesson.

The easiest instrument to play and one that is most easily adapted to variations of sound is the tambour. It can be beaten, using either end of a drum stick, the hand (using fist, fingers, knuckles), and it can be rubbed, brushed or tapped with the fingers. The wooden rim can also be used to produce a variety of sounds when tapped with the drum stick or the fingers.

Other percussive instruments perhaps have more limited use but add variety to accompaniment. A list of these, together with the type of movement they suggest, is given below.

1. Drum, including tambour .. thrusting and flicking movement.

2.	Cymbal and gong	..	..	sustained movement.
3.	Cymbals	..	..	sudden, strong movement.
4.	Clappers	..	..	angular, jerky, sharp movement.
5.	Triangle	..	..	light, sustained movement.
6.	Bells ..	..	..	shaking movement.
7.	Chiming bells		..	shaping of movement, change of level.
8.	Indian bells ..	..	..	sustained movement.
9.	Maracas	..	..	light, jerky movement.

The teacher's voice can make a natural accompaniment to dance. As well as telling the children what she wishes them to do, she can help the quality of their movement by the intelligent and expressive way she uses certain words. For example, the pitch of her voice will vary according to whether she wants a light or strong movement. Repetition of words stimulates the children to move in a particular way and can introduce phrasing and rhythm. Vocal sound, such as humming, whistling and hissing can also be used.

Records and tape recordings as an accompaniment

Records can often be used for the accompaniment of a simple dance or in the initial movement training. It is essential that the part of the record that is chosen is short so that the children can listen to it and become familiar with it. It is also essential that it is simple and clear to interpret. Some records are especially designed for dance accompaniment.

Tape recordings can be used in a similar way to records, consideration being given in the same way to simplicity and length. The recording can be made of a piece of music and repeated on the tape so that it can be danced a number of times. It can also be the recording of the children's vocal sounds or percussion made with a variety of instruments and objects.

Accompaniment by the children

As the children become more experienced in listening to various accompaniments and to dancing, they should be given the opportunity of making their own accompaniment. Ideally they should be allowed to handle different pieces of percussion and to discover the sounds they make when used in different ways. They could then fit suitable movements to the sounds. Limited use must be made of this experience due to the disturbance it may cause in the school, particularly if the hall is placed centrally. This idea can be modified and the class divided into groups, one child in each group being selected to play the instrument. She can 'try it out' while the rest of the group moves to her playing. After some experimentation, she should be encouraged to make up a phrase which she can repeat so that the group knows the accompaniment for their dance. As many children as possible should be given the chance to play.

EXAMPLE OF LESSONS

LESSON FOR A FIVE YEAR OLD CLASS

OPENING. (Use of space.)

Dance, travelling anywhere in the hall. Make patterns with your feet as you go; turn and twist; use all the space. (Teacher accompanies freely on the tambour.)

MOVEMENT TRAINING. (Body awareness.)

1. Sit on the floor, show me your feet. Make one foot dance in the air, make the other foot dance in the air. Now stand up and make your feet dance on the floor. Make them take you all over the hall.

2. Show me your hands. Make them dance round you. Dance with your hands as you travel about the hall. Make your hands dance near the floor and near the ceiling.

3. Now dance with your hands and feet making them go in all directions, sometimes low, near the floor and sometimes high, in the air.

CLIMAX. (Dramatic form.)

Dancing dolls. Make a shape like a dancing doll. Dance to another spot and stop in another shape.

(Teacher accompanies on the tambour introducing a simple phrase.)

LESSON FOR A SIX YEAR OLD CLASS

Movement idea—Spiky and smooth.

OPENING

Free dancing to accompaniment. (Piano, percussion or record.)
Try to dance with different parts of your body and use all the
space.

MOVEMENT TRAINING. (Body awareness and quality.)

1. Show me your hands—make them into a spiky shape.
Now make them dance with quick, spiky movements all round
you.

2. Make your feet spiky. Dance over the floor with quick,
spiky feet.

3. Dance with spiky hands and feet.

4. Make another part of your body spiky. Dance on the
spot/travelling with this part of your body spiky.

5. Make a spiky shape, dance to a new spot and make
another spiky shape.

6. Make a spiky shape dance with spiky movements to a new
spot and make another shape.

7. Repeat all or any of the above with contrasting smooth
movement. (Phrasing should be introduced wherever possible.)

CLIMAX. (Dramatic form.)

' Jack Frost '. The snow falls smoothly on the ground and
settles, freezing to a spiky shape. ' Jack Frost ' dances and
gradually melts away.

LESSON FOR A SEVEN YEAR OLD CLASS

Movement idea—Size of movement.

OPENING

Dance freely using all the space in the hall and then dance
using very little space.

MOVEMENT TRAINING

1. Dance from one spot to another sometimes using small
steps and sometimes using large steps. (The teacher's accompaniment should introduce simple phrasing.)

2. Run and leap showing small and large leaps according to
the accompaniment.

3. Curl up a little way and stretch out; curl up a little further and stretch again; then curl up tightly and stretch out as far as you can. (Rhythm.)

4. Reach out with your hands a little way and gather in; reach out a little further and gather in; then reach out as far as you can and hold.

CLIMAX. (Dance study.)

The children start grouped together in the centre of the hall, each one showing a curled shape. They dance opening out a little from the group and close in again. This is repeated reaching out a little further and closing in again. They then open right out, dance and enjoy the space in the hall and finish in the closed group again. (The phrasing of this will be guided by the accompaniment.)

BIBLIOGRAPHY

AGILITY

Educational Gymnastics. R. Morison. 2s.

Moving and Growing. (Physical Education in the Primary School. Part I)—Ministry of Education. 7s. 6d.

Planning the Programme. (Physical Education in the Primary School. Part II)—Ministry of Education. 7s. 6d.

THE OUTDOOR LESSON

Games activities for Girls. M. Dunn. 5s. 6d. Blackie & Son Ltd.

Physical Education in the Infant School. M. Laing. 12s. 6d. Arnold—Leeds.

P. E. Teacher's Handbook for Infant Schools. Julie Sharpe. 9s. 6d. Evan Brothers Ltd.

DANCE

Discovering Dance. Rachel Percival. 9s. 6d. London University Press.

Leap to Life. John Wiles and Alan Garrard. 15s. Chatto & Windus.

Modern Dance in Education. J. Russell. 11s. 6d. Macdonald & Evans Ltd.

Modern Educational Dance. R. Laban. 10s. Macdonald & Evans Ltd.

Music, Movement and Mime for Children. V. Gray and R. Percival. 15s. 6d. Oxford University Press.

Simple Guide to Movement Teaching. M. North. 12s. 6d. London—M. North.

Printed for Greater London Council Supplies Department by Waterlow & Sons Limited,
London · Dunstable · Hyde 11000 (73661) 6/66 505348   Binding by James Burn Ltd.